Paleontology:

Digging for Dinosaurs and More

by Laura Johnson

PEARSON

Scott
Foresman

Editorial Offices: Glenview, Illinois • Parsippany, New Jersey • New York, New York
Sales Offices: Needham, Massachusetts • Duluth, Georgia • Glenview, Illinois
Coppell, Texas • Ontario, California • Mesa, Arizona

ISBN: 0-328-13538-0

3 4 5 6 7 8 9 10 V0G1 14 13 12 11 10 09 08 07 06

What Is Paleontology?

Paleontology is the study of living things that died before people kept records. If none of these living things are around today, how do we know they once lived? Through the study of fossils!

Fossils are preserved, or saved, remains that offer proof of plant or animal life from long ago. There are two types of fossils. One type is body fossils. These are remains of body parts, such as bones, that have been preserved over the years. The second kind is trace fossils. These are clues left behind by animals, such as footprints, tracks, and bite marks.

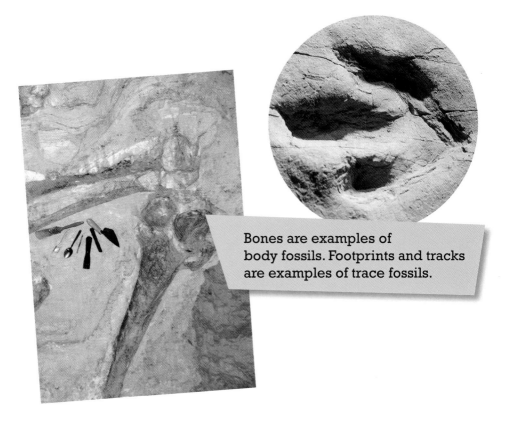

Bones are examples of body fossils. Footprints and tracks are examples of trace fossils.

From Bones to Fossils

Fossils can form when plants and animals die and fall to the ground. Plants and animals die all the time, but fossils are rare. This is because conditions must be perfect for a fossil to form.

Let's look at how a fish can become a fossil.

1. First, the fish dies in a place where there is little air, such as the bottom of the ocean. Or it dies at the surface and sinks to the bottom.

2. Minerals in the water work their way into the fish's bones and body parts. After a long time, all the bone in the skeleton is replaced by minerals that harden and turn into stone.

3. Layers of mud, sand, clay, and rock build up on top of the skeleton. Their weight presses down. Over many years, the pressing causes the layers to stick together and form rock.

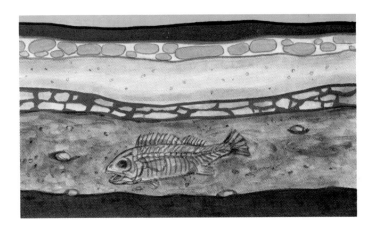

4. The fish is now preserved in solid rock. If the fossil is discovered and studied, it will provide clues about the fish that once lived.

Preparing Fossils for Display

Putting together an animal's fossils to create a museum exhibit is very difficult! Most fossils are too delicate to be put on display. Instead, replica, or look-alike, bones are used.

To make replica bones, workers create a **mold** of each fossil bone. The mold is created by painting a bone with layers of a rubbery material. After the material dries, workers peel it away from the bone.

Next, the mold is filled with either plastic or plaster. When this material hardens, the mold is peeled away. There is now a replica of the bone. The replica is painted to look like the original fossil. Sometimes, if a fossil skeleton is not complete, workers need to create replacement parts. The replacement parts must be in the right **proportion** to the rest of the bones.

When the painting is finished, the replica bones are ready to be connected in the shape of the animal. Workers build a frame to support the rebuilt skeleton. The frame is arranged to show how the animal stood.

Once the frame is **erected,** paleontologists lay out the replica bones and arrange them correctly. Starting at the **foundation,** the bones are attached to the frame. Then the model is ready for display!

A worker creates a mold of a dinosaur skull.

The Finished Product: Sue

One of the most famous fossils is a *Tyrannosaurus rex* named "Sue." Sue was named after fossil hunter Sue Hendrickson. She discovered the fossils in 1990. Sue is the largest, most complete, and best preserved Tyrannosaurus rex yet discovered. Of the more than 250 bones in a *Tyrannosaurus* skeleton, only one foot, one arm, and a few ribs and back bones are missing from Sue.

It took six paleontologists seventeen days to excavate the fossil of Sue. Then, it took a group of ten workers two years to clean the bones and piece them together!

You might be asking, do paleontologists ever make mistakes when they make models of extinct dinosaurs? Sometimes they do. The first replica made of a dinosaur was a model of an *Iguanodon.* When scientists first pieced its bones together, they decided that one of the bones was a horn. Years later, other scientists realized that that bone was not a horn. It was a spike on the dinosaur's thumb! On another **occasion,** the head of one kind of dinosaur was attached to the body of a different dinosaur.

Sue can be seen at the Field Museum in Chicago, Illinois.

More Recent Discoveries

Paleontologists have known for a long time that most plant-eating dinosaurs were bigger than their meat-eating relatives. For a while they thought that the largest plant-eating dinosaur was *Brachiosaurus.* This huge dinosaur was about 90 feet long and weighed roughly 75 tons. In 1979 fossil hunters in New Mexico discovered fossils of an even larger plant-eater. They named it *Seismosaurus*, meaning "earth-shaker." This dinosaur may have been 120 feet long and may have weighed nearly 90 tons!

Using computer technology, some paleontologists have decided that *Seismosaurus* could move its tail faster than the speed of sound. There is one thing we know for sure about the tail of *Seismosaurus*: It was huge!

It would take five school buses lined up end-to-end to equal the length of *Seismosaurus*!

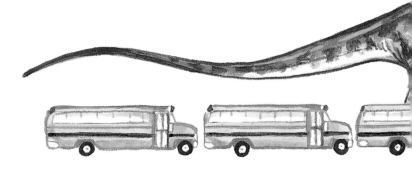

In 1996, scientists in China found a fossil skeleton of a small dinosaur that they named *Sinosauropteryx*. The fossil had feather-like markings.

Up until then, scientists thought all dinosaurs were cold blooded. The discovery of what might be feathers on the *Sinosauropteryx* fossil meant that some dinosaurs may have been warm blooded. Warm-blooded animals include

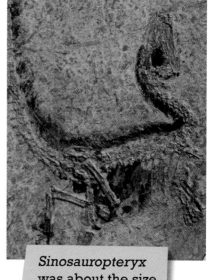

Sinosauropteryx was about the size of a turkey.

birds and mammals. If dinosaurs were warm blooded, then they would have been able to adapt to changes in temperature. For cold-blooded animals, such as frogs, lizards, and snakes, the temperature of their blood changes with the temperature of their surroundings, so they can easily get too hot or too cold.

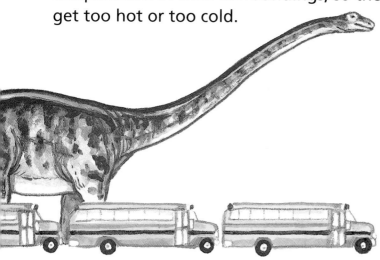

Recent discoveries have led scientists to change their minds about how dinosaurs behaved. Paleontologists once thought that dinosaurs did not form groups or care for their young. However, a set of newly discovered fossil footprints shows that some dinosaurs lived in groups and took care of their young.

These footprints were found in Colorado and Texas. They show both small and large footprints made by the *Apatosaurus*. The prints seem to show that parents and young dinosaurs traveled together.

Sue Revisited

Computer images of the inside of Sue's skull show very large olfactory bulbs. These bulbs control an animal's sense of smell. Scientists used to think that *Tyrannosaurus rex* had a poor sense of smell. But the images suggest Sue had a good one!

Most scientists believe that *Tyrannosaurus rex* was mainly a hunter. But this new information suggests that it might also have been a scavenger. Scavengers are animals that eat dead and decaying creatures.

So did Sue spend most of her time hunting or scavenging? New information often presents more questions than answers!

Apatosaurus lived in what is now Colorado and Texas.

In 1985 many dinosaur bones were found in Alaska.

Most dinosaurs lived in hot climates, but new discoveries have shown that this wasn't true of all dinosaurs. In 1985 fossils of eight types of dinosaurs were found in Alaska. Alaska is very cold today, so scientists wondered how dinosaurs could survive there. However, when they studied the fossils of plants as well as of dinosaurs, they discovered that Alaska was much warmer millions of years ago.

There are still some questions. Though Alaska was warmer then than it is today, it was still cooler than places where most dinosaurs lived. Scientists are still trying to find out how Alaska's dinosaurs adapted.

What Happened to the Dinosaurs?

There are several theories about what caused dinosaurs' extinction. At different times scientists thought that volcanic eruptions, diseases, or a gradual cooling of Earth might have been the cause. Now, however, most scientists believe that the effects from a huge asteroid hitting Earth caused the dinosaurs to become extinct.

You've now learned about how paleontology works and what paleontologists do. You've also read about the new ideas that have developed as new dinosaur fossils have been found. One thing is for sure: We will keep learning more about dinosaurs as scientists find more dinosaur fossils!

A huge asteroid hitting Earth may have been responsible for the extinction of dinosaurs.

Glossary

erected *v.* to have been put up straight; to have set upright

foundation *n.* the part on which the other parts rest for support; base

mold *n.* a hollow shape that you pour soft or liquid material into that gives its shape to the hardened material

occasion *n.* a particular time

proportion *n.* a proper relation between parts

tidied *v.* to have put in order; to have made neat

workshop *n.* a building or area where work is done